This Journal Belongs to :

Made in United States
North Haven, CT
24 March 2022

17524491R00057